Year 1

# called
Discussion Guide

## Shiao Chong

FAITH
ALIVE®
Christian Resources

Grand Rapids, Michigan

# Acknowledgements

This study is part of *Disciples,* a comprehensive multiyear faith formation program for adults.

The first year of *Disciples* consists of five studies of five weeks each:

- Follow Me
- Called
- Created
- Crafted
- Commissioned

Subsequent years will build on this foundation to help churches produce wholehearted disciples of Jesus Christ.

Supplementary materials for leading and participating in this study are available at www.GrowDisciples.org.

We gratefully acknowledge the following source on which this study and this series are based: *The Bible's Teaching on Discipleship* by David Holwerda, Emeritus Professor of New Testament at Calvin Theological Seminary, Grand Rapids, Michigan. This comprehensive, yet concise theological work surveys and collates both Old and New Testament teachings on the topic of discipleship. It is not in print but we encourage you to read it. It is available without cost online at www.GrowDisciples.org.

We welcome your comments. Call us at 1-800-333-8300 or e-mail us at editors@faithaliveresources.org.

ISBN 978-159255-404-1

10 9 8 7 6 5 4 3 2 1

# Table of Contents

# Introduction

How does one become a disciple of Jesus Christ? The familiar adage "Disciples are made, not born" emphasizes, rightly, that discipleship takes effort, learning, and commitment—it does not happen automatically. Simply being born into a Christian family does not mean that one will become a disciple of Jesus. And didn't Jesus commission us to "make disciples" (Matt. 29:19)? But thinking of discipleship only in this way hides an even more important truth: that disciple-making is, first and foremost, God's work, not ours.

What are some mistaken tendencies when we focus on discipleship *making*? The usual answers for how one becomes a disciple involve first making a choice to follow Jesus and then performing the right disciplines, such as Bible study, daily devotions, prayer, memorizing Scripture, worship, and, of course, following Jesus in our everyday lives. None of these are inherently wrong or mistaken. But to focus on this *first* in discipleship is to focus on the wrong thing.

When I was first learning how to drive, my instructor kept telling me to look at where I was going. "Eyes before wheels," he would say. That means two things. First, always look before you go, which is a good rule for safety. But second, where we focus our eyes usually determines where we are steering. Our hands tend to steer in the direction we are looking. So if we focus sideways, we inadvertently tend to drift to the side, even when we think we are keeping the wheel steady. If we focus on the wrong direction, we will drift, even unintentionally, in that direction.

Disciple *making* focuses us on the process, the "how to" of discipleship. If that's our *only* focus we will drift spiritually toward depending on our own strengths and devices, our own willpower and discipline to make ourselves disciples of Jesus Christ.

Disciples are made. But first they are *called*. By focusing on calling first, we recognize that it wasn't our choice or commitment that set us on the journey of discipleship; it was Jesus' call to follow him that got the ball rolling. By focusing on calling, we see that the whole discipleship process is a dialogue with God through Jesus Christ— God calls, we respond; God calls again, we respond further, and so on. Every step we take in the discipleship journey is not simply the fruit of self-discipline but an act of obedience and response to God's initiative, God's calling, God's teaching and guidance. By focusing on calling, we also focus on the fact that disciples are followers. It is not a spiritual self-help program. Discipleship is follower-ship, following where Jesus calls us to go. Finally, by focusing on calling rather than making, we also recognize the great privilege and responsibility of discipleship.

Imagine that one day you get a phone call from the President of the United States or the Prime Minister of Canada. He or she asks you to join the administration and help make the country a better place. How would you respond? How would you feel? Most of us would probably feel privileged and honored. Most of us would simultaneously be scared or anxious about the enormous responsibility entrusted to us in this call.

## Word Alert

In the Reformed and Presbyterian tradition we say that ministers are **called** to a church. Of course they have a choice, and the wise "calling" congregation looks at them very closely before calling. But it's more than being interviewed and taking a job. It's responding to a call—of a congregation and ultimately of God. Our tradition also emphasizes that we all live "called" lives. In secular terms we have a vocation, which comes from the Latin for calling. The word church in Greek is *ecclesia*, which means "called out." All this points to the mysterious truth that who we are and what we do somehow begins with God.

Discipleship is God, the Creator and Lord of the universe, calling us by the Holy Spirit to join the great mission of reconciling all things to himself through Christ Jesus. It is a great honor but also a great responsibility. We cannot take this calling lightly. It takes commitment, effort, and hard work. And it is not like a

## Web Alert

Be sure to check out our web page, www.GrowDisciples.org. It includes suggestions for group leaders plus all kinds of links and interesting stuff for exploring Jesus' call in your life.

New Year's resolution we may take up at will. It's an awesome call that we obey.

# Session 1

## Called by Jesus

## Ice Breakers
*(15 minutes—give or take)*

This is our first session, so please **take some time to get acquainted.** Distribute blank 3 x 5 cards and draw an object or animal or combination that tells something about yourself you don't mind others knowing about. Don't worry—artistic skills are not necessary! When everyone has drawn their artwork, go around and share the drawings and explain how the drawing represents something about you. It can tell a story in your past or explain a role you currently have or a personality trait or achievement you are proud of.

### Option
If you prefer to save a tree, just go around the circle and introduce yourselves. Do include a brief, fun story of when you did something you really wished you hadn't done.

## For Starters
*(10 minutes)*

Now that you've introduced yourselves, **page back and read through the Introduction on pages 5-6**. Read it on your own or assign a reader.

**Briefly discuss** this question: What caught your attention or surprised you in the Introduction?

## Let's Focus

*(2 minutes)*

**Read this focus statement together:**

The first question in understanding discipleship is not "What do I need to do?" but "Whose voice do I hear?" Before we look at what we are called to do, we need to first look at who is calling us. We are called by God, but more specifically, we are called by Jesus Christ. How important is it for our discipleship to realize that it begins with God rather than with something we can do ourselves?

## Word Search

*(20 minutes)*

**Read aloud the following Scripture passages and briefly discuss the questions under each one.** (You probably won't have time for all of them, so you may want to pick out the ones you especially want to cover, or just do as many as time permits.)

- Mark 1:16-20
  Do you think Jesus had ever met these men before? (*Hint:* See John 1:35-42.)

  Is it significant that Jesus meets Simon, James, and John in their daily work?

  What does it mean to "fish for people?"

  What was their response? Do you think they ever went fishing in the Sea of Galilee again?

---

**Word Alert**

Maybe you've heard the hilarious old Abbot and Costello routine "Who's on first?" In the Reformed tradition we're always concerned about what comes **first**. When you boil it down, the mysterious doctrine of election basically means that what God does always comes before what we do. God's grace, God's love, God's call, God's gift of faith come first. Everything else is response.

---

**Another Angle**

"Jesus furnishes his invitation with an exciting promise. It is the promise of catching persons, of being effective with people. . . . At the epicenter of our being, more central than even the sex drive, is the desire to influence others. We are socially constituted to make a mark. Jesus promises that mark. 'I will make you fishers of people.'"

—Frederick Dale Bruner, *The Christbook, Matthew 1-12*, Eerdmans, p. 127

- Luke 5:27-32

  What's significant about Jesus calling a tax collector to be his disciple?

  What does Jesus' attendance at Levi's party tell us about following Jesus?

- John 15:15-16

  Jesus calls his disciples his friends. What's the difference between a servant and a friend?

## Bring It Home
*(15 minutes)*

**‑( Word Alert )‑**

**Tax collectors** were deeply despised by many Jews in Jesus' day. Essentially they worked for the Roman occupiers to extort taxes from their own people. Since they got to keep whatever was left over, they tended to collect much more than was required. An equivalent of a tax collector today would not be an IRS or Canada Revenue agent but a fraudulent mortgage lender or a mafia kingpin.

**Choose one of these options:**

## Option 1

**Distribute paper and drawing implements of your choice. Choose *one* of the three passages and draw what you imagine your relationship to Jesus is like based on that story.** (Are you still holding the net, reluctant to go to the party, or wondering where you lost control of this thing?) Again, don't worry if you can't make a living as an artist!

**Share with each other what you drew and why.** Remember, there are no right or wrong answers to this exercise. We do not judge each other's answers but listen attentively to learn from each other and to learn about each other.

## Option 2

**As time permits, choose from among these questions and discuss them,** or formulate your own. Give each other the opportunity to answer but don't put anyone on the spot. For those who are not yet ready to toss out their thoughts, silence is golden.

- Do you find the stories of Jesus calling his disciples comforting, disturbing, confusing, or frightening? Why or why not?

- Are there some things you left to follow Jesus or things that still need to be left behind? Briefly describe what these are and why they are hard to leave.

- Jesus is interested in sinners, not the righteous (Luke 5:32). How does that affect what your discipleship looks like? Your church's calling?

- Do you feel like a friend of Jesus? Why or why not?

## Option 3

Have someone **read Luke 5:27-31** again slowly and thoughtfully, pausing after each sentence or image. As the passage is being read, have all the members of the group imagine the scene in their own minds. At the end of the reading, allow a few moments of silence for the group to complete their imaginary place in the story. Then **invite group members to share what they imagined, saw, or felt.**

- Who did you identify with in the story?
- Where were you in the scene? A participant, an onlooker?
- What did you imagine Jesus looked like—his expression, his demeanor?
- Did this story inspire you to be a disciple of Jesus? Why or why not?

# Pray It Through

*(10 minutes)*

**Take time to raise items to pray about together:** items for praise, thanksgiving, confession, or request. Also invite group members to mention struggles with their own discipleship for which they would like prayer. Pray in whichever way your group feels most comfortable: one or more persons praying, popcorn style, asking people to pray for the person on the left or right, or however the Spirit leads you. You can also choose to use the following prayer structure for this session or for other sessions:

**Opening Prayer (either a leader prays or the group prays together)**

O Lord, you are our light and our salvation. To you we pray and ask for your Spirit to be with us. You call us to be your disciples. May we hear your voice and follow you with all our hearts. You have promised that where two or three are gathered in your name, you are there in the midst of them. May we, therefore, know your holy presence among us now, and hear us even as we pray to you, our Lord and Savior Jesus Christ.

**Prayer Items (at this point, pray for the items that were raised)**

**Closing Prayer (pray the Lord's Prayer together or the following prayer from St. Patrick)**

Christ be with me, Christ before me, Christ behind me,

Christ in me, Christ beneath me, Christ above me,

Christ on my right, Christ on my left,

Christ where I lie, Christ where I sit, Christ where I arise,

Christ in the heart of every one who thinks of me,

Christ in the mouth of every one who speaks of me,

Christ in every eye that sees me,

Christ in every ear that hears me.

Salvation is of the Lord!

May thy salvation, O Lord, be ever with us. Amen.

*(The Breastplate of Saint Patrick, c. 373-463)*

# Live It Out

*(All next week)*

Disciples are called by Jesus, but often that call comes through significant people in our lives. **This week think about a person or persons who helped you hear Jesus' call, served as a spiritual mentor, or helped shape your path of discipleship. Consider writing a note thanking** that person for what he or she did for you. If you wish there *could* be such a person in your life, make it a matter of prayer every day.

> **Web Alert**
>
> Be sure to check out www.GrowDisciples.org for tips and follow-up reading for this session.

# Session 2
## Called to Follow Jesus

**Warmly welcome anyone who is new to your group. Briefly review** by summarizing your last session so that newcomers won't be left in the dark.

In the Introduction, we compared God's call of discipleship to a call from the President or Prime Minister asking us to join the administration for the good of the country. Seeing discipleship in this light should fill us with both a sense of honor and a feeling of awe at the enormous responsibility we have been called to. The more important the calling, the more commitment, risk, and personal sacrifice are required of us. That's certainly true of being Jesus' disciples, and Jesus never tried to hide it. In fact, we might sometimes wish Jesus had toned down his all-too-pointed descriptions of the rigors of discipleship.

Today many churches market themselves as the place to meet your needs, make your family happy, and find personal fulfillment. They draw attention with signs featuring cute sayings or lush promotions. By contrast, imagine Jesus' own words on a church sign: "Come join us. Sell all you have and follow Jesus." Or "Deny yourself so you can find your life."

In this session we are going to look at the demands Jesus makes of those who answer his call and follow him. It's not easy to be a disciple, but the risks are rewarding. The demands of discipleship will shape you into the character of Christ. Most important, it's

> **( Word Alert )**
>
> **Marketing** has found its way into churches too. And why not? There's nothing wrong with marketing itself. In one sense marketing is merely bringing people's attention and shaping their desire for a product (in this case, faith in Jesus Christ). It's another word for evangelism. On the other hand, it's not that simple. Marketing tends to use symbols and images that hook people on what's being sold (think the Nike swoosh). Jesus' attraction was the depth of his character and the authenticity of his call, not the coolness of his image.

the most exciting and fulfilling life you can live because it represents God's wonderful reign right here and now.

## For Starters
*(10 minutes)*

Last session you were asked to think about people through whom you heard Jesus' call to discipleship. Some in the group could talk about a mentor or spiritual guide who embodied Jesus' call to discipleship for them. Wonder together what made these people attractive and influential.

## Let's Focus
*(5 minutes)*

**Read the opening paragraphs of this session aloud or for yourselves, then have a volunteer read this focus statement aloud:**

Disciples are committed to follow their Master unconditionally wherever he goes. There are two actions in such following: (1) we leave something behind, and (2) we follow despite uncertainties and difficulties. Hence, disciples of Jesus must count the cost of following. Jesus calls his disciples to follow him knowing the sacrifices, risks, dangers, and uncertainties.

## Word Search
*(20 minutes)*

**Read aloud the following Scripture passages and discuss the questions under each one** (or formulate a better question of your own).

- Luke 14:25-33

  Why did Jesus use such strong language as "hate" (as in hating one's own family and even one's own life) in order to be his disciple? (compare Matt. 10:37) How would you put it into your own words?

  Do you think that Jesus was literally asking his followers to give up all their possessions to follow him?

Summarize in one sentence the main point you learned from this passage about following Jesus.

- Mark 8:27-38

What was wrong with Peter's picture of Jesus as Messiah? In what ways might we have a similar problem today?

What, in practical terms, might it mean in your life to deny yourself?

Summarize in one sentence the main point you learned from this passage about following Jesus.

| Word Alert |

In everyday speech we sometimes exaggerate to make a point: "The combination of that tie and sport coat makes me sick." Jesus used exaggeration rather freely in his teaching too, as when he spoke about **hating one's family.** In this case, he doesn't mean we are to hate family in an emotional sense, and certainly not as a matter of principle, but that when a choice is demanded by circumstances, everything, even family, takes a back seat to our commitment to Jesus.

# Bring It Home

*(15 minutes)*

**Choose one of these options:**

## Option 1

Divide into pairs and **chart out what the journey of discipleship might look like** on a piece of paper. First draw a line from left to right across the paper and label it "Called by Jesus." The left is the starting point of the discipleship journey. Then mark different points along the line (journey) and give them labels. For example, you can label the end point as "Arrive at the New Jerusalem!" Maybe there's a "moment of truth" along the way. Think of your own experience of discipleship on this timeline and try to incorporate what you have learned from today's Bible passages. As time permits, **share your timeline** with the group.

## Option 2

**As time permits, choose from among these questions and discuss them, or formulate your own questions.** Give each other the opportunity to answer, but don't put anyone on the spot.

- What does "carry your cross to follow Jesus" mean to you? How is your cross similar to Jesus' cross? How is it different?

- What has following Jesus cost you? What are the payoffs? Is there always a cost in discipleship?

- How would you tell a person who was considering discipleship about the rigors and rewards of following Jesus?

┌─ Word Alert ─┐

*The Cost of Discipleship* is the title of a powerful book by Dietrich Bonhoeffer, a theologian and pastor in Germany during the Nazi era who was hanged by the Nazis just before the end of the war. In that context, Bonhoeffer's title points to the fact that especially at certain times and places, following Jesus can be very costly indeed. Yet as Bonhoeffer was led out of his cell to be hanged, his last words were these: "This is the end . . . for me the beginning of life."

## Option 3

This option is delightfully off-beat and takes some preparation beforehand. **Find a CD with the old pop song "I Will Follow Him" in advance and listen to the song.** (A good version is the one in the movie *Sister Act* with Whoopi Goldberg. You may be able to get a CD of the movie soundtrack from the library. Otherwise, rent the movie and cue the DVD/VCR to the part near the movie's end where the song occurs.) If you can't find a CD, then find the lyrics of the song via the Internet. Listen to (or read) the lyrics carefully and **discuss whether this secular song of a woman's love for her man can be seen as a song of Christian discipleship!** Why would this song be fitting or why not?

# Pray It Through

*(10 minutes)*

**Share your prayer requests together. Then pray in whatever way is most meaningful for your group.** You can use the prayer structure at the end of session 1 again if you wish.

Even better, let group members suggest one or more ways in which they struggle with the cost of being a disciple of Jesus, and invite the group to pray for each other in these struggles.

## Live It Out

*(All next week)*

**Find a nail, preferably one with a little heft, and carry it with you this week. As you do, reflect on sins or other hindrances in your life as a disciple that you need to "die to"**—in other words, that you need to nail to the cross as a follower of Christ. List some steps you need to take to make

that happen. Pray and commit those actions to the Lord. If you are comfortable, share your commitment with a spiritually mature Christian (a mentor perhaps) to keep you accountable over the long haul.

> **Web Alert**
>
> **Be sure to check out www.GrowDisciples.org for tips and follow-up reading for this session.**

# Session 3

## Called to Imitate Jesus

Take a few minutes to **get up to speed as a group.**

In our last session we learned that disciples are called to follow Jesus. One of the shades of meaning that the word "follow" takes on is *imitate* or *copy*, as in following a pattern or model. So to be a disciple means not only to travel the Way Jesus leads us but also to copy or to imitate Jesus as our model for how to live in relation to God, to others, and to God's creation.

In this session **we will explore how and in what ways we can imitate Jesus.**

> ### Word Alert
>
> Today it's so easy to copy: think photocopies, digital copies, mp3s, file sharing. In fact it's so easy the media industry is trying to find every legal or technological way to stop it: that's what copyrights are for. But there's no copyright on Jesus Christ. God hopes to flood the world with authentic copies of the one true human being. In Jesus' case, imitation truly is the sincerest form of flattery.

## For Starters

*(10 minutes)*

Last week the group was invited to carry a nail to remember the cost of discipleship. Perhaps some group members are willing to share a thought or experience that "nailed down" the costliness of discipleship for them.

## Let's Focus

*(5 minutes)*

**Read the introduction to this session. Then have someone read this focus statement aloud:**

Imitating Jesus is not simply a superficial mimicking. When disciples imitate their master they *identify* with him. Another image that may help is that of an apprentice. The apprentice carefully watches the master until the master's actions become second nature to the apprentice. To imitate Jesus is to identify ourselves with him so much so that we become Christ's presence, Christ's body in this world. To imitate Jesus also means to follow Jesus' example of self-sacrificial servanthood.

**┌─ Word Alert ─┐**

Many trades involve an apprenticeship—often several years of working alongside the master—watching, assisting, and finally doing it yourself. It involves learning the craft and the language that goes with it (the apprentice bricklayer, for example, needs to learn what it means to "frog mud"). Think about the interesting implications of discipleship as an apprenticeship with Jesus.

## Word Search

*(20 minutes)*

**Read aloud the following Scripture passages and briefly discuss the questions under each one** (or formulate a better question of your own).

- John 13:12-17
  What is the example Jesus sets here for his disciples?

  What does washing "one another's feet" mean for you today?

- Philippians 2:5-13
  Assuming that "have the same mind" means imitate, what does Paul call us to imitate?

  Jesus did not use his equality with God "to his own advantage" (TNIV). What might you be using to your advantage as a Christian? What does following Jesus' example mean in that case?

How does God's "working in you" relate to Paul's invitation to "work out your salvation"?

- Philippians 3:15-17
Here Paul invites his readers to follow the example of his own life and that of other mature Christians. Why is that an important addition to following the example of Jesus?

If we are to *make* disciples as well as *be* disciples, must our life be an example?

# Bring It Home
*(15 minutes)*

**Choose one of these options:**

## Option 1
Discipleship and apprenticeship have some common characteristics. **Design an "apprentice of Jesus" program** together. Decide on the steps, the skills that need to be learned, the common language to be mastered, and the length of time needed.

## Option 2
**Discuss these questions.**

- Discuss some ways in which discipleship is like an apprenticeship. For example, learning the language of the trade, learning by doing, the goal of being a "journeyman."

- In what ways is it exciting and daunting to be imitators of Christ?

- How do you react to the idea of being an example for others to imitate as Paul so freely offered himself? What aspect of your life would you offer to someone for imitation? Does it demand perfection?

**Word Alert**

It seems odd and maybe vain to invite others to imitate us. But it's important if we are to make disciples of others. It doesn't mean we're perfect. It means we're inviting them into our joys, struggles, and yes, even failures, as we seek to follow Jesus.

## Option 3

**Break into two teams and play an impersonation form of charades.** Have each group plan an impersonation of a Bible character and then act it out with words or dialogue if you wish (let your imagination run wild!). Let the other team guess who you're portraying. When they have guessed it correctly, the group should **say a few words about what an imitation of that Bible character would entail.** (Act that out too if you are creative enough and if you have time.)

# Pray It Through

*(10 minutes)*

**Invite members of the group to take a few moments for reflection and then share** a concern, a desire, or a problem concerning their imitation of Christ or the example of their own life, which you can then bring to the Lord as a group. Then **pray in whatever way is most meaningful for your group.** You can use the prayer structure at the end of session 1 again if you wish.

# Live It Out

*(All next week)*

**Pray, reflect, and discern one attitude, behavior, or action of Christ that you wish to imitate this week.** Also be aware of a person or persons you have consciously imitated, whether in good or bad ways. Try to be specific: what, when, where, how? Be prepared to tell the group about your experiences with imitation in your next session.

> **Web Alert**
>
> Be sure to check out www.GrowDisciples.org for tips and follow-up reading for this session.

# Session 4

## Called to Learn from Jesus

**Warmly welcome each other back and do a brief review of the last session.**

Imitation is one of the most fundamental ways of learning. As a child you learned by imitating your parents or your older siblings. You tried to talk by parroting what you heard. You learned to play by watching how older children played. You learned by imitating others.

Disciples are called to imitate Jesus because they need to learn from Jesus. First-century Jewish disciples often learned from their rabbis the "tools of the trade" so that they could become rabbis too. But disciples of Jesus never become masters themselves. We never become independent of our Lord Jesus. Disciples of Jesus

**Word Alert**

**Rabbi** is Hebrew for "teacher" or someone who was distinguished in knowledge. The authority and recognition of being a rabbi didn't come with a diploma from a rabbinical seminary but from the grassroots recognition of others who desired to become a rabbi's disciples (see Matt. 7:28-29). In the Judaism of Jesus' day, rabbis were the main interpreters of the law for matters of everyday life: How far may one walk on the Sabbath? What is a proper tithe? Both Jesus' disciples and his enemies called him a rabbi. The term explains the many instances in which Jesus was embroiled in interpretations of the Jewish law.

are perpetual learners, perpetual followers, and perpetual imitators. Even disciples who become leaders in the church or Christian community are still followers and learners of Jesus. If we ever lose the spirit of humility and teachability, then we lose our identity as disciples.

What must disciples learn from Jesus? Let's take a closer look.

# For Starters

*(10 minutes)*

At the end of the last session you were asked to try to imitate an attitude, behavior, or action of Jesus; or observe how you tend to imitate others. As much as you are comfortable, **share your experiences and observations with the group.** Remember, we are all learners, not experts in discipleship!

# Let's Focus

*(5 minutes)*

**Read the introduction to this session. Then have someone read this focus statement aloud:**

As we learned last time, an important aspect of discipleship is imitating Jesus and those who walk with Jesus. But disciples also learn and grow by applying what Jesus taught to their lives. Jesus said, "Go and make disciples . . . *teaching* them to *obey* everything I have commanded you" (Matt. 28:19-20). Disciples learn to do what Jesus teaches and obey what Jesus commands. In the Sermon on the Mount (Matt. 5-7), Matthew gathers many of Jesus' teachings into one exciting lesson. In it Jesus radically reinterprets the law without taking anything away from God's commands: "You have heard it was said. . . . But I tell you. . . ." Disciples today still go to the school of Christ to learn how to follow him.

# Word Search

*(20 minutes)*

**Read aloud the following Scripture passages and briefly discuss the question(s) under each one (or formulate a better question of your own).**

- Matthew 11:28-30

  What are some reasons why people may be "weary and burdened"? What do they need rest from?

  What characteristics of Jesus make learning from him easier or less burdensome? What do you think it means to be yoked to him?

> **Word Alert**
>
> **Yoke:** a wooden bar or crosspiece held across the shoulders for carrying a pair of pails or over the necks of two oxen to pull a plow or wagon. Ancient Jews spoke of carrying the yoke of God's law or the yoke of his kingdom. It was an image of obedience.

- Mark 12:28-34

  In this episode, a teacher of the law momentarily became a student of Jesus. Do you think his question has any connection with being "weary and burdened" (Matt. 11:28)?

  Where does Jesus' answer come from? (*Hint:* See footnotes in Scripture text.) Why is that important?

  If this teaching is an example of Jesus' "yoke," would you find these two commandments "easy" and "light"? Why?

- Mark 4:1-9

  In this parable Jesus the teacher holds up a mirror to his students. What kind of soil describes your situation right now?

# Bring It Home

*(15 minutes)*

**Choose one of these options:**

## Option 1

And now for something completely different! Get a hymnal and look up "What a Friend We Have in Jesus." **Work together to create an additional stanza that emphasizes learning from Jesus,** perhaps using some of the ideas and images of the passages above. Maybe it can even rhyme! Then sing it together.

## Option 2

**Discuss as many of these questions as time allows:**

- Disciples are called to take on Christ's yoke and to learn from him. How does being yoked to Jesus comfort or challenge you? How does it help you learn from him?

- Christ promises that his way gives us rest for our souls. Have you found that rest? How?

- In the story in Mark 12, Jesus said that the teacher of the law was "not far from the kingdom of God." Why do you think Jesus said that?

- The teacher of the law asked Jesus which, of all the commandments, is the most important one. Why do you think Jesus gave two commandments instead of only one?

- List some examples of loving God with all your heart, soul, mind, and strength. (It might be interesting to see if you can come up with specific examples for each.) Then list some examples of loving your neighbor as yourself.

## Option 3

Our Lord Jesus used "yoke" as a metaphor for obedience and learning. **Either search around in your immediate room/home/building or brainstorm for another object to symbolize the act of learning from Jesus.** You can choose to do this either as a group or as individuals. Whichever way you choose, make sure you take some time to discuss why you chose the particular object. Why is it an appropriate symbol?

# Pray It Through

(10 minutes)

**Invite members of the group to share one thing they're in the process of learning from Jesus, or something that they'd like to learn more from Jesus. Then pray in whatever way is most meaningful for your group.** You can use the prayer structure at the end of session 1 again if you wish.

## Live It Out

*(15-25 minutes each day during the coming week)*

**Web Alert**
Be sure to check out www.GrowDisciples.org for tips and follow-up reading for this session.

One of Jesus' major teach-ins is the Sermon on the Mount. **Each day take time to read, pray, and reflect on Jesus' teachings in Matthew 5.** Take notes on whatever you have learned from your daily readings. Reflect on how you can apply or respond to what you have learned. Be prepared to **share with the group what you have learned** during your next session.

# Session 5

## Called to Be Citizens of God's Kingdom

**Warmly welcome each other** to the last session of this second study in the *Disciples* series. Do a quick review of your previous sessions to orient you to today's topic.

When I became a Canadian citizen back in 2000, I was given a certificate of citizenship that solemnly reminded me that I was now "entitled to all the rights and privileges of Canadian citizenship and . . . subject to all the obligations and responsibilities of . . . citizenship." Citizenship has its privileges but also its responsibilities.

Each country has a set of principles or values its citizens are expected to uphold. For instance, as a Canadian I was asked to "uphold the principles of democracy, freedom and compassion, which are the foundation of a strong and united Canada."

As Jesus' disciples, we are citizens of the kingdom of God. Like our national citizenship, citizenship in God's kingdom has its privileges as well as obligations. As disciples, we are called to follow Jesus' Way by imitating and learning from him. The Way of Jesus is the way of the kingdom. Sometimes that meshes with our earthly citizenship, sometimes it doesn't. That potential conflict may sometimes get Christians into trouble, just as it got Jesus into trouble.

God's kingdom is much bigger than any human kingdom or government and is much bigger even than the church. God's kingdom embraces all of life, all of

**( Word Alert )**

Jesus' teaching was all about king-dom. The first words out of his mouth in the gospel of Mark were "The kingdom of God has come near . . ." (Mark 1:15). The concept of kingdom doesn't translate into North American culture very well since we don't have monarchies (though we do have some notable political dynasties). It might be helpful to think of kingdom in terms of God's government, the regime of Christ. Jesus reasserts God's rightful claim on the world he has made. And he gives notice to the powers of this world that a new regime has begun—a new King has come.

creation, and claims it for the Lord Jesus Christ. The kingdom is right here and right now, but it embraces the future too. It will come in its fullness when Christ returns to usher in a "new heaven and a new earth." You can't be involved in anything bigger or more exciting than the kingdom of God.

## For Starters

*(10 minutes)*

At the end of your last session you were asked to reflect during the week on part of Jesus' Sermon on the Mount. **Share notes on what you have learned from Jesus this past week.**

## Let's Focus

*(5 minutes)*

**Read the introduction to this session. Then have someone read this focus statement aloud:**

Disciples are called by Jesus to be citizens of God's kingdom, to embody kingdom virtues, and to join God's great mission of reconciliation. In this way, disciples live under the kingdoms and governments of this world but their ultimate loyalty is to God's kingdom and to the Lord Jesus Christ. In the midst of evil and competing loyalties, Jesus' disciples are called to remain true to God's rightful and loving claim over all his creation.

## Word Search

*(20 minutes)*

**Read aloud the following Scripture passages and briefly discuss the question(s) under each one (or formulate a better question of your own).**

- John 18:33-38
  What did Jesus mean by saying "My kingdom is not of this world? (*Hint:* He explains it further by saying "my kingdom is *from* another place.")

  What does this have to do with Jesus' assertion that his followers would not fight for him?

What does it mean for you and your involvement in the world to belong to a kingdom not from this world?

- Matthew 6:31-34

What causes people to worry? How does our seeking "first [God's] kingdom and his righteousness" alleviate that worry?

- Luke 17:20-21

What does Jesus mean when he says "the kingdom of God is in your midst?" How do you see or experience it?

# Bring It Home
*(15 minutes)*

**Choose one of these options:**

## Option 1

**Work together on drawing a simple diagram of the relationship between the church and the kingdom of God.** How would you visualize the church's relationship to the kingdom?

## Option 2

**Discuss these questions:**

- What are some of the ways in which you might live out your kingdom citizenship in your everyday life as a disciple of Christ?

- How have you experienced conflict between your national citizenship or other obligations in this world and your citizenship in God's kingdom?

- In what ways does your citizenship in God's kingdom lead you to be involved in this world or to turn your back on it?

## Option 3

Pretend that you are being sworn in as citizens of God's kingdom. What would your "pledge of allegiance" sound like? Brainstorm ideas, and then craft a pledge of allegiance and say it together. If there's time, consider writing lyrics for a "national anthem" or choose one from popular Christian hymns or songs. If you prefer, do the anthem option instead of the pledge of allegiance.

## Pray It Through

*(10 minutes)*

Jesus taught us to pray, "Your kingdom come . . . on earth as it is in heaven." **Share some of the specific ways you desire God's kingdom to come in your life, your church, your community, your world, and then pray about them together.** Close by praying the Lord's Prayer together. Or you can use the prayer structure at the end of session 1 again if you wish.

## Now What, Now Where?

Since this concludes this second study of what it means to be a disciple of Jesus, you'll have to **decide what happens next:**

- You can choose to tackle the next five-session study in the *Disciples* series: *Created*. Be sure to set the time and place for your next session.
- If you wish to study something else, agree together on what that will be. (Check out www.GrowDisciples.org for more resources on the kingdom of God and www.faithaliveresources.org for lots of excellent ideas for more small group studies.) Again, be sure to agree on where and when you'll meet next.
- If your group needs modification, appoint two or three trusted persons to work with other small group leaders to make the required changes. They'll want to consult with your church leadership and/or your pastor to work out a new plan. Prayerfully commit to joining revised/new groups that may result.

## Live It Out

*(As long as it takes)*

In our Introduction, we imagined getting a call from the President or Prime Minister inviting us to join in the mission of running the country. We reflected on the honor, privilege, and awesome responsibility of such a call.

As Jesus' disciples, we have been called by our King. King Jesus calls us as citizens of his kingdom to join in his mission of reconciling the world to God, of showing and spreading the Way of life and righteousness. It is a glorious calling with great responsibility.

It is now time to ask, **How do you answer the call of Jesus? What commitment(s) do you need to make in response to Jesus' call?**

Write down these commitments and share them with your spiritual mentor to keep you accountable. If you don't have someone with whom you regularly talk and pray about your spiritual journey, consider finding such a person. Pray that God will lead you to a mentor and ask your church pastor or elder for help. Then take the opportunity to regularly revisit and pray over these written commitments. Intentionally keep them as part of your discipleship calling to be good kingdom citizens and ambassadors for God.

**Web Alert**

Be sure to check out www.GrowDisciples.org for tips and follow-up reading for this session.